Getting the best out of Think Through History

The principles of Think Through History emerge straight from successful classroom practice. The pupils' books and supporting resources have been written by experienced teachers who know how to set and achieve the highest possible standards in historical knowledge, understanding and skill for all abilities. The authors believe that three main principles must underpin successful learning:

● motivation

● rigour

● appropriate pace.

Pupils must be engaged by the material (motivation), they must be directed towards focused and demanding targets (rigour), and they must be helped with clear, structured stages including plenty of opportunity for checking, revisiting and reinforcement (appropriate pace).

Using Think Through History to motivate pupils

When curiosity, fascination or wonder is caught, learning accelerates. Lower attainers, especially, need to be drawn in if they are to sustain the effort necessary to embrace a complex historical idea or to recall some necessary information. Each Enquiry in Think Through History is built around the structural principles which make a good history lesson. Just as the start of each lesson is crucial to gathering and exciting the pupils' attention, so each Enquiry begins with a powerful draw. Whether it is an arresting source, a dramatic landscape, a disturbing story, a puzzle, or the enticement of a really absorbing activity to come, the inspirational teacher must be equipped with the 'Wow!' factor to prepare pupils for an interesting historical journey.

Many teachers have found that books in which short sources proliferate lack a clear storyline to help pupils get started. Think Through History re-enthrones narrative – the missing teaching tool. Thus pupils can build a more robust and memorable understanding that will help them to pull more aspects of their historical learning together.

The use of story is deliberately inventive, often adopting a particular voice. In Enquiry 2, the complexities of life in London around 1600 are set before the eyes of two foreign visitors, each of whom responds differently. In Enquiry 3, the burgesses of Bristol are seen struggling over a period of a hundred years or more as they try to strike a balance between helping the poor and punishing them. In Enquiry 9, the pupils are deliberately asked to see the period between 1642 and 1660 as years of 'madness', as one contemporary called them. Through these approaches the difficult ideas in past attitudes, beliefs and values (so vital for the political, social and cultural understanding) are made accessible and meaningful to lower attaining pupils.

In order to maximise the motivational power of Think Through History, teachers should, wherever appropriate:

● read aloud short passages of text, whether source or story, with lively or exaggerated intonation

(The humour in 'Monarchs in their place' (Enquiry 10) and the pain and frustration of the brothers in 'A thing most horrible' (Enquiry 8) need to be drawn out so that even weak readers feel the power and contrast of contemporary attitudes.)

● make full use of the 'Think' questions.

(These devices also help to *mediate* the text for pupils. The 'Think' questions can be used as starting points for purposeful whole-class questioning or else as checking and reflection devices for pupils while they read through the text on their own.)

Using Think Through History to make challenging work achievable

When planning a sequence of lessons, it is so important to make sure that the learning journey 'goes somewhere'. Each Enquiry in Think Through History concludes with an activity which has a significant and worthwhile outcome. Pupils need the satisfaction of knowing that they have completed a substantial and meaningful activity. Teachers need to be confident that the time spent on the activity developed real period understanding and historical skill.

The sequence of STEPs in each Enquiry makes the final activity possible. The STEPs place a strong emphasis upon helping pupils to select and order their ideas. In this way, challenging tasks are enjoyable and realistic.

All history teachers know the danger of the 'fun' activity – poster, play or cartoon – which actually yields anachronism, unhistorical flights of fantasy or a wasted half-hour spent colouring in. The final activities in each Enquiry keep the fun, but build in checks to secure the rigour.

A wide variety of final activities is used throughout Changing Minds:

Enquiry	Final activity	Enquiry	Final activity
1	A diagram which shows the relationship between the different sources used and questions raised by pupils in the Enquiry	7	Notes for a speech by a Privy Councillor whose experience of advising Elizabeth I has to be used to tell James I how England is governed
2	A role play which draws on observations made on life in London from the perspective of an optimist and a pessimist	8	A card-sorting exercise in which pupils take events mentioned in a play and group them to analyse the causes of the Civil War
3	A one-minute radio broadcast in which pupils support their interpretation of how poverty was dealt in this period	9	A cartoon which pupils draw or describe to show some aspect of life between 1642 and 1660
4	An analytical essay explaining and illustrating the way in which historians may reach different interpretations even though they have used the same source material	10	A balloon debate in which pupils draw on their knowledge of how six monarchs ruled the country
5	A letter in which pupils use what they have learnt about life on the Anglo-Scottish borders to warn a new warden for the area of the dangers he will face	11	A Danger Chart which pupils create to show times of religious persecution between 1547 and 1603
6	A simple, structured booklet aimed at telling an audience of primary school children about the Henry VIII's Break with Rome	12	Thought bubbles reflecting the contrasting values and beliefs of colonists and Native Americans
		13	An analytical essay in which pupils organise their insights into the causes of the witch-craze
		14	A chart which reveals the common strands in the work of four important 17th-century scientists

Using Think Through History to build knowledge

Teachers of history always aim to avoid superficial coverage. Instead, they must build layers of knowledge and conceptual understanding which will last after the smaller, factual details have been forgotten. This is not best achieved with rapid, fact-crammed 'outline' studies. Where overviews are used these need to be revisited and drawn upon so that pupils come to see the point of acquiring a particular layer of knowledge or 'outline' understanding. Think Through History blends overview and depth just as the creative teacher would.

Depth adds illustrative colour and memorable drama to broader, outline issues. Overviews ensure that depth studies are seen in context, yielding more period-sensitive questions in pupils.

Teachers using *Changing Minds* to plan a Study Unit should note the following features:

- **'Overview' Enquiries** which use humour, macro-stories and lively prose in order to make 'big' stories and themes memorable (for example, the kings and queens who return from the dead to tell their tales in Enquiry 10).

- **'Depth' Enquiries**, short in-depth elements within Enquiries and Enquiries which offer structured frameworks for further depth studies (for example, the setting of religious changes in England and Wales within the wider European context in Enquiry 11 or the framework for the analysis of different types of source in Enquiry 1).

- Deliberate **blending of 'overview' and 'depth'** in creative interplay (for example, Enquiry 3 gives an in-depth understanding of the story of the poor in Bristol, but this acts as an example of the development of social legislation and the relations between rich and poor).

Using Think Through History to make planning easier

The good teacher does not imagine that a single mention of a fact or idea will be enough to drive it home. Pupils need to climb into a difficult issue in lots of different ways until they have made sense of it. *Changing Minds* helps them do this on two scales. Instead of following a rather lifeless, information-giving structure, each Enquiry carefully and subtly revisits themes through repetition of vocabulary, steady building of an idea and lots of backward looks to check that certain pupils have not got lost – just as a teacher would.

Likewise, on the scale of the whole book, there is ample opportunity for the building of big themes. These are indicated by the Enquiry titles and their key questions. The 'minds' theme is strong throughout because all history involves making sense of individual motives and institutional ideas in difficult and strange contexts. But all sorts of other themes can be woven in to support this. It is possible for teachers to build really interesting workschemes which allow pupils to see connections and threads through reinforcement.

All the Enquiries in Think Through History are self-contained. They will work on their own. Some teachers may wish to dip in and select certain Enquiries which complement other textbooks and resources. The Enquiries have also been designed so that linking and coherence across the Study Unit and across the whole Key Stage is made easier.

Here are two contrasting workscheme structures which meet the demands of the National Curriculum in imaginative and purposeful ways. The goal is to make the best use of the time to ensure *thorough knowledge and understanding* rather than the meaningless notion of 'content coverage'.

Route 1 – Three themes:
social change, political change and changes in culture and ideas

---

Life and death

1 **Dead and gone**
2 **'So famous a city'**
3 **Vagrants and vagabonds**
4 **A woman's life**
5 **'Revenge for revenge and blood for blood'**

}

- social structure and diversity
- views and attitudes of different groups
- evidential problems arising from attempts to enquire into 'hidden lives'.

With this sense of period in place, pupils are then ready to overlay it with a chronological 'map'.

Rule and rebellion

6 **Chopping and changing**
7 **Queen and country**
8 **'A thing most horrible'**
9 **'The maddest world we ever saw'**
10 **Monarchs in their place**

}

- experiments in control
- power structures and struggles
- motives for power and power bases
- the development of the monarchy.

Familiarity with key names, dates and events will supply pupils with a mental map or frame of reference. A careful balance and interplay of broad brush and fine detail (overview and depth) treatment will help pupils to understand and to enjoy the main narratives in limited available time.

Hopes and fears

11 **Forcing minds to change**
12 **Culture clash**
13 **Evil on their minds**
14 **'Words new and unheard of'**

}

- the power of religion over ordinary lives
- links between secular power and religion
- changing philosophical, religious and scientific ideas
- diversity of beliefs.

Route 2 – Two interlinked themes: change and continuity

Introduction

12 Culture clash

Use this Enquiry to introduce the power of ideas. To understand the past we have to understand what went on in people's minds. Here, two sets of minds differed so much that they could not possibly understand each other.

Tudor stories of change

6 Chopping and changing

7 Queen and country

11 Forcing minds to change

These three enquiries show enormous change taking place. Sometimes things changed in line with people's intentions. Sometimes they changed *despite* people's intentions.

Stuart stories of change

8 'A thing most horrible'

9 'The maddest world we ever saw'

10 Monarchs in their place

14 'Words new and unheard of'

Rapid and fundamental change took place in the Stuart period. Change occurred in the development of ideas and in institutional structures.

Continuity: what stayed the same?

3 Vagrants and vagabonds

Yet despite all this change, some fundamental attitudes were remarkably enduring. In the treatment of the poor, all sorts of changes occurred on the surface, but, at another level, nothing changed.

Continuity or change?

1 Dead and gone

4 A woman's life

5 'Revenge for revenge and blood for blood'

13 Evil on their minds

These four enquiries illustrate a mixture of continuity and change. The core political narrative is revisited as a background theme in Enquiries 5 and 13, thus helping to reinforce pupil's knowledge of chronology and key political changes.

In addition, *Changing Minds* can be used for whole-book navigation exercises in pursuit of particular themes. The following are ideas for the launch or conclusion of a scheme of work. They are also useful exercises for the teacher who is seeking to find alternative workscheme structures which serve thematic coherence and knowledge reinforcement:

● Use the Index in *Changing Minds*. Which words occur *most* often? What does this tell us about the period? What does it tell us about the themes within the book?

● Use the 'Key terms' checklists for each Enquiry which you will find in this Teacher's Book. These include the terms which the National Curriculum prescribes in **Key Element 5b**.

● Use the Enquiry titles on the contents page of *Changing Minds*. Can pupils spot the theme in 'Hopes and fears'? Can you draw their attention to the deliberate continuity and contrast in the key questions for Enquiries 7 and 8?

Using Think Through History to support historical enquiry

The processes and principles of historical enquiry are now a well-established tradition in school history. They are enshrined by National Curriculum **Key Elements 3 and 4**. Pupils must be aware of the problems involved in reaching historical conclusions. They must understand the conditions under which valid claims about the past can be made.

Think Through History places a strong emphasis upon this aspect of school history. It supports learning in this area in five ways:

1 All material, questions and activities are built around key questions. Each chapter of the book is openly styled as an Enquiry in pursuit of a solution to a carefully-defined and limited historical problem. The Enquiry titles model good historical questions – ones worth answering. Pupils are also helped gradually, across the four pupils' books, to frame significant historical questions of their own.

2 Each Enquiry is carefully structured. The authors do not use the word 'enquiry' to mean open-ended, unstructured investigation. The devices for gathering, sorting, sifting, weighing, criticising and synthesising information are all transferable and designed to *teach* pupils to become independent enquirers in the long-term. Pupils are helped systematically to *think* in purposeful, critical ways. Practice in recalling, selecting and arranging information, using tables, headings and diagrams, needs to become second nature until, by the end of Key Stage 3, pupils can tackle an historical problem with some independence. The key to successful training in historical enquiry is to get the balance between structure and independence just right.

3 Rather than attempting to address the 'reliability' question on every other page, particular aspects of evidential understanding are focused upon in certain Enquiries. For example, in 'Dead and gone' (Enquiry 1) pupils develop the skill of raising their own questions by considering different types of source. In 'A woman's life' (Enquiry 4) pupils see how influential the selection of source material is in arriving at or justifying an interpretation. In this way, strong, transferable understandings of the historical process are developed self-consciously and clearly.

In *Changing Minds*, the now hackneyed 'Is this source reliable?' question is used very sparingly. There is much more to evidential understanding than spotting 'unreliable' sources all over the place! Such questions often clutter up learning, because they have no obvious relationship to the particular learning purpose. In fact, such approaches tend, albeit unintentionally, to feed the mistaken impression that there is some right answer to be found if only enough 'truthful' sources could be obtained. Here and there, pupils are reminded of the need to think critically and reflectively about the provenance of a source, perhaps in a carefully positioned 'Think', but otherwise such issues are explored *only in those Enquiries where they are consistent with the chosen learning focus*.

4 Many modern, history textbooks give the impression that there is some rigid distinction between, on the one hand, 'the sources', and, on the other, the author's voice as some instrument of a heavenly intelligence transcribing official truths. An impression is thus created that it is the purported neutrality of the latter to which we are aiming. We all know that this is not really the case. Think Through History can be used to teach pupils, through example and challenge, that there are many types of historical truths and layers of meaning in differing interpretations. The authors aim, throughout, to give pupils a balanced understanding of the issues, sometimes acting as guide and commentator, sometimes as relaters of key stories. The following would be excellent questions to ask at certain stages in the books:

● Whose side are the authors on here?

● How balanced are the authors being here?

Whilst Think Through History re-enthrones narrative as a vital and motivating teaching tool, it also opens the way for critical reflection on its provenance.

5 Finally, the structure of each Enquiry is only a skeleton. It acts as a good framework for a short lesson sequence addressing a particular historical question. It is expected that teachers will use other resources in support of each Enquiry's principles. For example, television programmes and orthodox textbook accounts can be used to support the play in Enquiry 8; a range of primary and secondary sources can be used to build an analysis of the role of Cromwell and other aspects of the 'maddest world' (Enquiry 9).

Using Think Through History to help pupils to join up their thinking

Many pupils find history difficult because concentration difficulties, memory problems and the sheer unfamiliarity of the material make it hard for them to hold on to more than one idea at once. Drawing a number of points together, or simply choosing relevant items, therefore becomes prohibitively difficult.

The STEPs equip pupils to sort information out. The longer and more demanding activities at the end of each Enquiry are not simply sprung on the pupil after varied but unfocused reflection. The STEPs systematically work towards the final activity so that over half the work is done before pupils get there. Sometimes the STEPs show the pupils how to select, sort, classify and synthesise. Exercises in choosing, linking and grouping help pupils to make connections and to see big issues. Exercises in designing headings help pupils to discern core themes and to classify their ideas.

Using Think Through History to help pupils write at length

Extended writing is difficult because joined-up thinking is difficult! All of the strategies discussed above are helpful as training for extended writing. Pupils need to confront, self-consciously, the organisational problem at the heart of any historical enquiry:

● What fact (or evidence or idea) do I want?

● Where shall I put it?

Almost all of the Enquiries, even those where the final activity is not explicitly an extended writing task, will act as a useful springboard for extended writing. Each Enquiry encourages pupils to avoid aimless gathering and copying of information. Each Enquiry encourages pupils to find relevance and order.

In addition to problems of structure, most pupils need help with appropriate style and register in their writing, especially where formal essay writing is required. Some Enquiries (and some of the supporting copymasters) therefore offer 'sentence starters' or 'paragraph starters' which will help pupils to find the right language with which to link up their ideas.

Using Think Through History to provide access and challenge for pupils of all abilities

Think Through History makes differentiation possible through a scaffolded and inclusive approach. After completing the STEPs, pupils will be familiar with the material, and, in some cases, will have done the necessary selecting and planning required for the final task. The STEPs often repeat a particular format. This is deliberate. It helps lower attainers to think about the requirements of a task.

In addition, the copymasters help the teacher to plan for further differentiation. The vast majority of pupils will be able to attempt the final 'Thinking your enquiry through' activity, but lower attainers will sometimes need additional props to get them there. Higher attainers will need an additional challenge to make sure that they really develop and use additional knowledge or reflect at a higher level. For this reason, each Enquiry is supported with ideas for 'Extra access' and 'Extra challenge'.

The copymasters can never be exhaustive. 'Extra access' copymasters are examples of ways in which teachers can isolate residual difficulties and design support for pupils to overcome them. They help pupils to experience the satisfaction of the full, final task. 'Extra challenge' copymasters avoid gratuitous, bolt-on 'extension activities'. Instead, they feed into the core task of the Enquiry, ensuring that higher attainers' performance in that task is enriched through greater knowledge, conceptual understanding or a more complex organisational framework.

Using Think Through History to develop moral sensitivity and cultural awareness

Most history teachers are aware of the danger of distorting the discipline of history into a vehicle for teaching particular moral values. However, such dangers do not mean that history is bankrupt as a vehicle for moral development – far from it. History is vital and powerful in facilitating all kinds of moral development:

● the emotion and drama of stories from the past foster moral sensitivity and human sympathy

● atrocities and inhumanity induce moral outrage

● conflicts, tensions and dilemmas develop moral reasoning.

True empathy is grounded in much knowledge. As pupils build up a rich picture of the contextual factors which informed attitudes, beliefs, ideas and institutions, so they are increasingly able to identify with other people in situations different from their own. Teachers can link the Enquiries in Think Through History with their school's PSE or citizenship programme in all sorts of ways:

● use Enquiry 4 ('Vagrants and vagabonds') to help pupils to reflect on the difficulties for those in authority in balancing support for the poor with deterrence of laziness or crime

● use Enquiry 12 ('Culture clash') to open discussions about the rights and wrongs of colonial settlement. How can different cultures co-exist?

● use Enquiry 13 ('Evil on their minds') to consider 'witch-hunts' as a general phenomenon. Links can be made to bullying and persecution of minorities.

Using Think Through History to make assessment workable and useful

Since the review of the National Curriculum in 1995 teachers have been freed to organise assessment in whatever way they deem most helpful. The Level Descriptions provide an outline guide and are useful for broad judgements using several pieces of work across a term or so. They remind us that pupils make progress in history in an *integrated* way. For example, knowledge serves evidential understanding; awareness of the processes of enquiry are affected by the ability to sort and organise information. Everything connects. We are no longer required to devise artificial routes through discrete skills (the process that led to such distortion in task setting in the 1991 National Curriculum).

However, on a day to day, week by week basis, teachers need much more precise instruments than the blunt tool of the Level Description! Teachers will want to ensure that pupils are getting better at history. This will involve careful, systematic attention to particular learning objectives specified for each part of the scheme.

Sometimes teachers will want to assess a **very specific issue**:

> For example, the ability to tell the difference between the general and the particular (the 'big points' and the 'little points') in order to develop aspects of the understandings described by Key Elements 4a, 4b and 5a.
>
> Enquiry 1, 'Dead and Gone', would develop very specific skills in this area.

Sometimes teachers want to see how pupils are handling **several variables at once**:

> For example, a piece of extended writing where pupils will organise their knowledge of Tudor/Stuart social diversity, their ability to select relevant items only, their ability to tell the difference between general and particular and their ability to use evidence critically. This would develop understandings in just about *all* the of the Key Elements!
>
> Using Enquiry 4, pupils could develop and demonstrate the management of all of these areas at once.

Teachers are always assessing. Every single task set, be it oral or written, formally marked or informally checked, tells the teacher if pupils have understood and whether the degree of challenge was inadequate, excessive or just right.

However, from time to time teachers wish to *record* the results of such assessments in order to build up a comprehensive picture of pupil performance. All of the final activities in the Enquiries are ideal for this purpose. The teacher's notes accompanying each enquiry in this book indicate the main areas which the enquiry addresses. This will help the teacher to decide which particular aspect they wish to focus upon and so to choose the kinds of information they might like to record.

For example, at the end of Enquiry 7, teachers might choose to record how much pupils have remembered and understood about key developments in the exercise of Elizabeth's power and influence as a monarch. The activity is designed to demonstrate the degree of understanding pupils have gained. After careful teaching, and the use of 'access' and 'challenge' copymasters as appropriate, teachers might wish to record pupil performance in a precise, meaningful way.

There are lots of ways of doing this. In their mark books, teachers might want to use a mark out of ten, they might want to use a simple tick, cross or other code to indicate that a proper threshold of knowledge has been passed, or they might generate expected bands of performance which indicate what they need to know about pupil successes and difficulties. When assessing the activity on page 63, some teachers would use a scheme like this:

Band 1 – A good understanding (for Year 8) of the problems facing monarchs, with proper attention to detail and clear understanding of (and ability to apply) specific terms such as 'nobleman' or 'propaganda'.

Band 2 – Adequate understanding – general awareness of key trends and no major confusions.

Band 3 – Some awareness of the problems facing a monarch, but anachronisms, serious confusions or gaps still exist.

This helps the teacher and the whole department *to make the necessary decisions for future planning and teaching.*

It informs the teacher and enriches departmental debate about:

- which pupils need some re-teaching (either within this topic or at a future convenient moment in the workscheme)

- which groups of pupils might benefit from more focused, more prolonged or alternative strategies next time the workscheme is delivered

- whether or not the sequence of lessons leading up to the activity motivated and informed pupils sufficiently to make them ready for the task.

These are the kinds of things that make assessment useful. These are the kinds of things that teachers need to know. If the assessment is not totally meaningful and useful, *don't do it.*

Feedback to the pupil will depend on the department's own policy, but in terms of the teacher's mark book, the acid test is: *is it meaningful?* It is a good idea always to remember these golden rules when assessing history:

- Be precise about learning objectives. What did you want all pupils/some pupils to learn? Assess *that.*

- Avoid *mechanistic* linking to the Key Elements. It is more likely that a good activity will develop understandings defined by an *interplay* of the Key Elements, than a single Key Element in isolation. For example, the activity on page 73 will test pupils' ability to link and organise causes. (This is an interplay of Key Elements 2b and 5a.)

Most activities will (and should) be serving some understanding described by the Key Elements. But avoid rigid hoop-jumping exercises that purport to show that pupils can or cannot tackle one discrete 'skill' area. Mechanistic hoop-jumping exercises cannot prove that pupils 'can detect changes' or 'can extract information'. This is far too imprecise. 'Detecting change' or 'extracting evidence' goes on being challenging right through to degree level! Pupils need constant practice at exactly the same thing! The level of challenge usually depends upon the amount and type of *knowledge* that you are dealing with. Teachers need simply to identify or integrate those areas of understanding which they really want to teach and which the activity really will show. The 1995 National Curriculum reinstated professional judgement on this issue. We must use it.

Using this flexibility properly, teachers need never fear that they will not be improving pupil performance as described by the Level Descriptions! Rigorous, well thought-out, purposeful assessment is more likely to lead to a steady improvement in pupils' real performance than direct, mechanistic linking of individual tasks to the broad statements of the Level Descriptions which were not designed for this purpose anyway.

The final activities in each Enquiry of Changing Minds will give varied and systematic practice in all the Key Elements, and therefore ample assessment opportunities. Aim for carefully-structured planning, activities with obvious (well-articulated) learning challenge and highly-motivating lesson sequences built around good historical questions. Always check and monitor pupils' learning. Ask: did they meet your lesson objectives? In this way, assuming that all Key Elements are *genuinely* being addressed (and it would be hard to find a good sequence of history lessons that was not addressing them!) pupils will make very good progress and your assessment systems will be sufficiently precise and sensitive to monitor it.

Level Descriptions are for the end of the Key Stage in Year 9. They are 'best fit' descriptors and should only be used for portfolios of several pieces of work together with your own knowledge of the pupils' performance. Some schools do find the creation of 'benchmark portfolios' in Years 7 and 8 helpful, but never limit assessment to this process. A pupil might legitimately remain at 'Level 5' for two years and yet still be making excellent progress! You therefore need other, much more sophisticated and flexible methods for assessing real progress during that time.

Dead and gone

How can we learn about hidden lives?

The opening Enquiry provides an overview of early modern society (**Key Element 2a**). This is a fresh approach to historical enquiry as it requires pupils to frame questions and to think about the significance of different types of question (**Key Element 4b**). The development of this aspect of historical enquiry is too often left to chance. Teachers will have to emphasise that pupils are not being invited to answer the questions included, for example, in STEP 1.

The Enquiry is structured around a range of different sources (**Key Element 4a**) which shed light on the domestic environment, demography and crime. These are important themes in the social history of this period (**Key Element 2a**).

Teachers may, of course, want to introduce pupils to the terms *general* and *particular* in the context of *big* and *little* questions.

O━┓ Key terms

   nobles, gentry, middling sort, lower sort, yeoman, parish registers, inventories

---

Extra access

Low attainers should be able to do STEP 1 without further support but will benefit from time spent discussing the difference between *big* and *little* historical questions.

Copymaster 1.1 helps low attainers with STEP 2 by giving them some questions to sort (as in STEP 1).

Low attainers should be able to come up with their own questions in STEP 3 having had support at each earlier STEP.

Copymaster 1.2 simply provides the diagram frame for pupils to use. This allows low attainers to do the historical activity straight away without losing time drawing circles!

Changing Minds
Enquiry 1

STEP 1

STEP 2

STEP 3

Thinking your enquiry through

Extra challenge

Copymaster 1.3 provides high attainers with extra sources to consider at each of STEPs 1, 2 and 3.

The fact that sources are drawn from different dates and locations may be the basis for some *big* questions about typicality.

High attainers should be encouraged to see links between different sections when 'Thinking your enquiry through'.

It is likely that some high attainers may raise questions about the way sources should be used. This is, of course, a sign of healthy enquiry work, but they should be encouraged to keep a clear focus on questions about social life in the period 1500 to 1750.

Big questions and little questions about parish registers

These historians are looking at some parish registers.
All sorts of questions have come into their minds.
Read each question carefully.

Decide whether each question is a big question or little
question. Then copy it onto the list you started in STEP 1.

Add some more questions of your own if you can.

Who lived longer in 1650: women or men?

How long did Robert Bell live?

Did the population of Easingwold go up or down in 1650?

Did people usually marry someone from their own parish?

What made Francis Driffield die so young?

How many families lived in Easingwold in 1650?

Why did some people move away from their own parish?

Extra access 1.2

Your enquiry web

Thinking your enquiry through

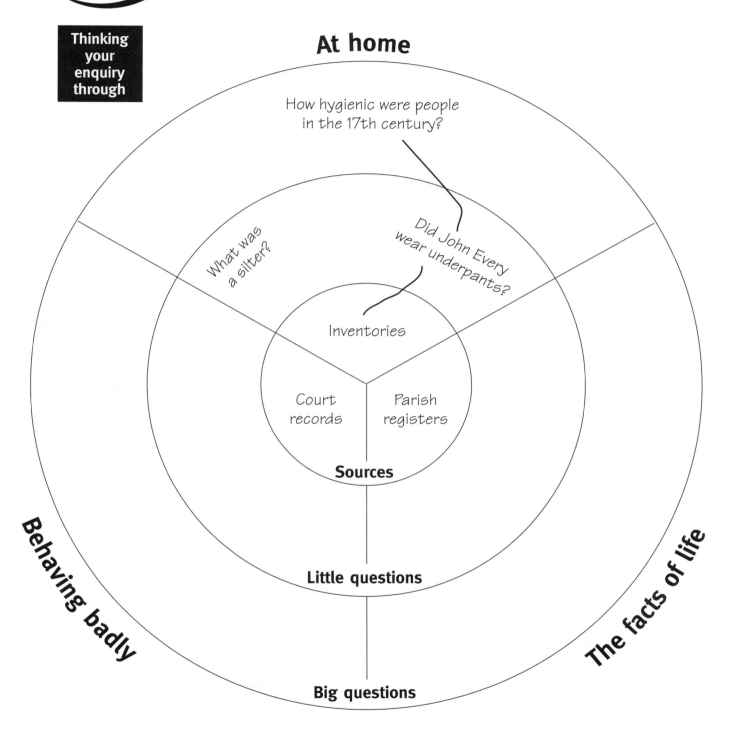

At home

How hygienic were people in the 17th century?

What was a silter?

Did John Every wear underpants?

Inventories

Court records

Parish registers

Sources

Little questions

Big questions

Behaving badly

The facts of life

Extra challenge 1.3

More sources ... and more questions

Use the extra information on this page to help you to think of some more **big** questions and little questions in each STEP.

STEP 1

An inventory showing some goods owned by Bennett Gue of Writtle, Essex, 21 April 1638

In the chamber	
– one feather bed and bolster,	£3-15s
Two pair of sheets	18s 0d
One brass pot	7s 0d
Two posnets (small cooking pots)	5s 0d
One chest	6s 8d
One salt box with other small things	12 d
In malt, 28 quarters – bushels	£60-4s
Six sacks	16s 0d
His wearing apparel	40s od
In money in his purse	£13-6-8d
In bonds & other good debts	£26-0-8d
In desperate debts	£6-0-0d
Debts due by him to others	10s 10d, 6s 8d
Total	£113-2-6d

[The appraisers wrongly calculated the total at £112-18s]

STEP 2

Information from the parish register of Crediton in Devon.

9 April 1571
– 5 people died of plague on this day.

18 June 1571
– By now 200 people had died of plague.
535 people died of plague in the whole year.

September 1591
– 36 people died of plague in this month.
One entry for September 1591 says that 'Isabell Reeve, a poor mayzed maide', died in the street and was buried with her clothing.

October 1591
– Over 80 people died of plague in this month.
There were only two normal deaths this month. One was of 'Joan Browne, wydowe by report almost 120 years having a son 84 years of age living'.

STEP 3

Information from the Quarter Sessions (criminal courts) for Devon in 1598.

At the Midsummer Assizes 1598 – 35 prisoners were on trial.

8 of the 35 were hanged. They had stolen sheep, clothes or cheese, or they had received stolen goods.

7 of the 35 were branded for stealing clothes and sheep-stealing.

13 of the 35 were flogged (including 6 women). They had either stolen sheep, clothes, cheese or had received stolen goods.

One man called John Knight was on trial for acquiring and using a 'love-charm which he used to cossen wenches with'. He was set free.

'So famous a city'

What was fine and what was foul in London life?

This Enquiry's central purpose is to build up a picture of the complex social network of London (**Key Element 2a**). It is rooted in a particular time (i.e. it is not about change) but the city is viewed through the eyes of two very different brothers. This device allows pupils to see how the same event or experience can produce very different opinions. Teachers may want to organise pairings so that lower attainers work alongside higher attainers as they gather information to use in the role play.

The STEPs require pupils to read carefully and *in role* so that the final role play should be informed and rooted in contextual understanding (**Key Element 2a, understanding attitudes**). Taking the roles of the two brothers also involves pupils in seeing how views from the past may have been affected by personal character or perspective (**Key Element 4a**). The pupils' own view of London life will also have been manipulated by being told to look for optimistic or pessimistic insights and so the role play also feeds understanding of interpretations (**Key Element 3a**).

> **⚷ Key terms**
> trade, merchant, optimist, pessimist

Extra access

Changing Minds
Enquiry 2

Extra challenge

Low attainers will probably cope better if the instructions from STEP 1 are given before they start to read through the first section. It is also likely that low attainers will find it easier to take on the role of the pessimist.

Copymaster 2.1 gives low attainers a grid with the main sub-headings of things to look out for in each section. (There are so many that no further help is needed, although the very weakest may benefit from being told to concentrate on a particular paragraph.) Pupils can record examples as they go along in STEPs 1, 2, 3 and 4. They can then use these to back up their views in the final role play.

STEP 1
STEP 2
STEP 3
STEP 4

Higher attainers should be encouraged to find lots of detail. (It is more challenging to look through optimistic eyes!) Close reading will reveal that the text is packed with opportunities. The challenge then becomes one of deciding what to leave out in the final role play!

Thinking your enquiry through

Everything in this Enquiry is based upon sources from the time but **Copymaster 2.2** provides more contemporary sources from which high attainers can draw information and make inferences.

After the role play, it may well be worth challenging high attainers to comment on what the exercise tells us about the benefits or dangers of approaching any enquiry with a fixed viewpoint (in this case optimistic or pessimistic).

What is fine and what is foul?

In this enquiry you have to take the role of one of the two brothers who are visiting London. Decide whether you are an optimist (who always finds good things to enjoy in life) or a pessimist (who only seems to notice problems). Write down which one you are in the box below.

I am _____

At each STEP in the enquiry, note down any fine or foul things about London on the grid below. (Remember – only put fine things if you are an optimist. Only put foul things if you are a pessimist.)

The River Thames	
Buildings	
Streets	
Trade	
Noise	
Crowds	
The treatment of foreigners	
Entertainment	
Safety	

Eye witness accounts of London

These accounts by people who saw London around 1600 give you extra details about what was fine and what was foul in the city.

1 Thomas Dekker describes London in 1606.

> In every street, carts and coaches make such a thundering as if the world ran upon wheels. Posts are set up to strengthen the houses, lest with jostling one another crowds should shoulder them down. Hammers are beating in one place, tubs hooping in another, pots clinking in a third, water tankards running at tilt in a fourth. Here are porters sweating under burdens and merchant's men bearing bags of money. Pedlars (as if they were at leap frog) skip out of one shop into another. Tradesmen are lusty at legs and never stand still.

2 The Lord Mayor of London complains about the theatres in 1597.

> Theatres contain nothing but profane fables and scurrilous behaviours. Plays move people to imitation and not avoiding those vices which they represent. Theatres give opportunity to evil-disposed and ungodly people that are within and about this city to assemble and carry out their lewd and ungodly practices. Vagrant persons, thieves, horse stealers, whoremongers, cozeners, coney catchers and other dangerous persons meet to the hurt and annoyance of Her Majesty's people.

3 Paul Hentzner, a foreign visitor, comments on the theatres in 1598.

> Outside the city are some theatres, where English actors represent almost every day comedies and tragedies to very numerous audiences. These are concluded by a variety of dances, accompanied by excellent music and the excessive applause of those that are present. At these spectacles and everywhere else the English are constantly smoking the Nicotian weed which in America is called Tobaca. They draw the smoke into their mouths and puff it out again through their nostrils, along with it plenty of phlegm and defluxion from the head.

4 Donald Lupton writes about London's many ale-houses in 1632.

> The hostess of an ale-house must be courteous to all, though not by nature, yet by her profession. For she must entertain all, good and bad, tag and rag, cut and long-tail. She suspects tinkers and poor soldiers most, not that they will not drink soundly but that they will not pay readily.

5 Fynes Moryson, a traveller who wrote about London in 1617.

> The houses of the citizens are very narrow but are five or six roofs high. There are many stately houses scattered in back lanes and streets which if they were joined together, as other cities are built uniformly, they would make not only fair streets but a beautiful city.

Vagrants and vagabonds

Did life change for the beggars of Bristol?

This Enquiry offers an overview of the treatment of poverty (**Key Element 2c**). There is a special depth focus on Bristol. The Enquiry explores reasons for change and continuity (**Key Element 2b**) in developments from the Elizabethan Poor Laws (with an emphasis on 1601) to the late 17th century.

It is questionable whether change was the most important characteristic of the long-term picture. It might be argued by some historians that very little changed at all in the attitudes of the rich to the causes of poverty and therefore that their policy is character-ised by continuity. This is the puzzle set to the pupils.

Throughout the Enquiry the teacher's aim should be to help pupils to realise that their decision about change and continuity is not straightforward. Knowledge is steadily built and reinforced in order to support this. The focus is on the ideas, beliefs and actions of elites (another facet of **Key Element 2b**). The Enquiry is drawn together in an interpretations exercise (**Key Element 3**) with carefully worded contending statements to crystallise pupils' choices between change and continuity.

> **Key terms**
> the poor, poverty, deserving poor, law, burgess, mayor, taxation, rate, parish, workhouse, change, continuity

Extra access

Changing Minds Enquiry 3

Extra challenge

Low attainers will find **Copymaster 3.1** helpful throughout the Enquiry. Not only does it provide prompts for pupils to consider at each STEP, it also puts these on a timeline (not to scale). It can form the basis of their first task in 'Thinking your enquiry through' as well.

Copymaster 3.2 helps pupils with their one-minute radio interview by giving them a question and answer framework.

STEP 1

STEP 2

STEP 3

Thinking your enquiry through

The challenge offered in **Copymaster 3.3** involves pupils in relating the experiences of the Bristol burgesses to the bigger, national picture of how the elite coped with poverty. This is done by giving them a summary of national developments as seen by a leading historian. Pupils must check this against the change and continuity they have noticed in their Bristol Enquiry.

Pupils could do this at the end but it would also work if they were to be given the historian's summary at the outset of this Enquiry. They could then check which statements can be supported by examples from Bristol at each stage.

Helping the poor and punishing the poor

The words below tell you what happened to poor people at the date shown. If you think the sentence is an example of people helping the poor, copy it under the heading 'How some of the poor in Bristol were helped'. If you think the sentence shows that people were punishing the poor copy it under the heading 'How some of the poor in Bristol were punished'.

In each STEP try to find some more examples of how the poor were helped or punished. Your copy of *Changing Minds* tells you where to look.

STEP 1

The 16th century

In **1586** the law said vagabonds could be whipped or have a hole bored in their ear.

In **1586** the law said vagabonds could be made to work as servants.

STEP 2

1601 to 1605

The **1601** Poor Law said churchwardens had to make unemployed people work.

In **1601** rich people had to pay the Poor Rate, which was a tax to help the poor.

In **1601** disabled poor people were given some money from the Poor Rate.

In **1601** anyone who refused to work was put in a gaol or a house of correction.

In **1601** vagabonds were whipped and sent back to their own parish.

STEP 3

The later 17th century

In **1680** all Bristol's parishes shared the cost of paying money to the poor from the Poor Rate.

In **1696** Bristol built a new workhouse where all fit, unemployed poor people were made to work.

In **1696** people who refused to work in the workhouse were whipped.

Extra
access
3.2

**Thinking
your
enquiry
through**

The interview

In the gaps on this sheet write in what you will say in your
radio interview.

Interviewer Good evening, professor. We are here to discuss your new book
Beggars, Burgesses and Beadles in Bristol. Please start by giving us
a summary of whether you think the treatment of the poor in
Bristol changed or stayed the same.

You Certainly. I have studied the beggars of Bristol very carefully and it
is my opinion that … _____

_____

_____

(Base your answer on either Statement 1 or Statement 2 on page 31 in Changing Minds.*)*

Interviewer I see. What made you reach this conclusion?

You There were several reasons. In the first place I noticed that …

_____

_____

(Now give one reason why you chose Statement 1 or 2.)

Interviewer Very interesting. Were there any other reasons?

You Oh yes. For example … _____

_____

_____

(Now give at least one more reason why you chose Statement 1 or 2.)

Interviewer Well, you certainly have thought about this. Is there anything you
would like to add?

You _____

_____

_____

(Try to add another comment of your own about what changed or stayed the same for the poor.)

Interviewer Well, thank you professor, but I'm afraid we must stop there.
Good night everyone.

Extra
challenge
3.3

**Thinking
your
enquiry
through**

What an expert thinks

In your radio interview you have to speak as if you are an expert on the
beggars of Bristol in Tudor and Stuart times. The words below were
written by a historian who has become an expert on beggars all over
England at that time.

Read the extract and compare what this historian says with your own
ideas about the beggars of Bristol. You can use some of his ideas in your
radio interview – but only if you have examples from Bristol to back
them up.

> The development of the vagrancy laws suggests that those who
> ruled Tudor and Stuart England were able to make effective
> responses to serious social problems. Many vagrancy policies
> were inhumane and repressive while some, such as the houses of
> correction, failed in their purposes. Yet in many ways those
> policies were successful. To those in power, vagabonds were a
> threat to the established order, and ultimately that danger was
> avoided. Those in power adapted old laws to the needs of the
> time, greatly expanding its range and the means to enforce it.
> The country gentlemen who dominated the House of Commons
> and local government found useful allies at parish level among
> the prosperous men. In addition to controlling vagrancy, they
> enforced poor relief and significantly eased the lot of the needy.
>
> Obviously, by comparison with today, the lives of the poor
> remained desperately harsh in seventeenth-century England.
> But, compared with other countries of that time, England's
> ruling elites [*highest groups*] did manage to take effective action
> on the social front. High-mindedness and charity may well have
> motivated them in part – but so, no doubt, did their
> determination to keep their own power.

Adapted from A L Beier, Masterless Men *(Methuen, 1985)*

A woman's life

How can historians disagree when they are working with the same sources?

This Enquiry helps pupils to develop an understanding of the lives of married women (**Key Element 2a**). It takes a new approach to historical interpretations by demonstrating how historians can produce different interpretations, even when they use exactly the same sources (**Key Element 3a**). Teachers may want to draw parallels here with Enquiry 2.

Pupils use some lively source material (**Key Element 4a**) in each section, extracting information from text or pictures to support one or other of two interpretations introduced at the beginning of the Enquiry (**Key Elements 3b and 5c**).

```
O—π Key terms
      interpretation, support
```

Extra access

Changing Minds
Enquiry 4

Extra challenge

Low attainers probably need an extra opportunity to reinforce the difference between the two historians' interpretations. **Copymaster 4.1** serves this purpose and it can then be used at each STEP to remind low attainers of the differences.

The 'Think' activities should make the STEPs accessible to low attainers as they are so closely related to the STEPs. As a further support, **Copymaster 4.2** can be used at each STEP. The teacher might simply give out the appropriate cards at each STEP and ask pupils to sort them and copy them onto their own list. Or they could all be handed out and cut up at the end and be used as a card-sorting exercise to help plan the final essay in 'Thinking your enquiry through'.

Introduction

STEP 1

STEP 2

STEP 3

STEP 4

Thinking your enquiry through

High attainers should be asked to consider extra sources as provided on **Copymaster 4.3**.

Higher attainers should be expected to develop the final paragraph in their essay. Here are some word prompts which they could be given. They would then have to devise sentences which use these words to explain why historians differ and find examples from the Enquiry to support the case. The words are …
• facts/opinion
• missing sources/new sources
• different places/different classes
• typical/atypical examples

The two interpretations

Here are the two historians shown on page 33 of *Changing Minds*. Read their different interpretations and then do the tasks below.

Introduction

Interpretation 1

Married women in the 16th and 17th centuries had a very hard time. Wives had to obey their husbands. They were often treated badly. Wives were not free to do as they wanted. They spent all their time looking after their husbands and children.

Interpretation 2

Married women had a lot more freedom than you think. Men and women were often equal partners in marriage. Husbands usually treated their wives well and women did not always obey their husbands. Married women did a lot of different jobs as well as looking after their families.

1 Underline all the words in Interpretation 1 which show clearly what this historian thinks about women's lives.

2 Now write a sentence which sums up Interpretation 1 in a simple way.

3 Underline all the words in Interpretation 2 which show clearly what this historian thinks about women's lives.

4 Now write a sentence which sums up Interpretation 2 in a simple way.

Sorting what the sources say

STEPS 1, 2, 3, 4

Men should have power over their wives (*Domestic conduct book*)	A Somerset woman beat her husband when he did not look after their baby properly (*From a plaster picture*)
Men should never hit their wives (*Domestic conduct book*)	Samuel Pepys used to hit his wife and insult her (*From a diary*)
Men should take advice from their wives (*Domestic conduct book*)	Adam Eyre got his wife to promise to obey him (*From a diary*)
Men are stronger and wiser than women (*Domestic conduct book*)	The wife of Samuel Pepys used to hit him and insult him (*From a diary*)
A husband and wife will not do well if they are not honest with each other (*Advice manual*)	Susan Eyre did not allow her husband to sell her land (*From a diary*)
Women spent time putting on their make-up as well as working hard (*Advice manual*)	Husbands usually left everything to their wives in their wills (*From a historian's findings*)
English wives go walking, riding and playing cards with their husband's permission (*A description by a foreigner*)	The law said that women had to give everything they owned to their husbands as soon as they got married (*From a historian's findings*)
Wives in England are under their husband's control (*A description by a foreigner*)	Court records show that men were sometimes brought to court for beating their wives (*From a historian's findings*)

More sources about married women

1 From Fynes Moryson's *Itinerary*, written in 1617.

> English husbands have great power. Their wives can neither give anything in life or make a will at death, nor can call anything their own – not so much as their garters! The law permits the husband in some cases to beat his wife. And yet the husbands treat their wives with all respect and with all honour. For the most part the husbands would carry burdens, go on foot, fast and suffer anything so their wives might have ease, ride, feast and suffer nothing.

2 From John Ray's *Collection of English Proverbs*, written in 1670.

> It is worth noting that in no country of the world are the men so fond of, so much governed by, so wedded to their wives as they are in England. Yet hath no language so many proverbs which are rude about women.

3 From a description of London by Frederick, Duke of Wurtemberg, in 1592.

> English women have much more liberty than perhaps in any other place. They also know well how to make use of it, for they go dressed out in exceedingly fine clothes, and give all their attention to their ruffs and stuffs. Many a one does not hesitate to wear velvet in the streets, which is common with them, whilst at home perhaps they have not a piece of dry bread.

4 From a letter written by Lady Mary Verney to her husband Ralph in 1649. Ralph wanted the boy to be called Richard – but Mary ignored him and had the child christened Ralph!

> If our child be born a boy, I am resolved to have it of thy own name, Ralph, therefore I charge you do not contradict me … I will be governed by thee in anything except the name if it be a boy.

5 From a letter by Ralph Verney to a friend in 1649. He is discussing his wife, Mary.

> I blush at her boldness but more at my own folly but you know she wears the breeches and will do what she wills.

'Revenge for revenge and blood for blood'

Why was life so wild in the Anglo-Scottish borders?

One aspect of this National Curriculum unit that pupils find difficult to understand and that teachers find dry to teach, is the constitutional relationship between England, Ireland, Scotland and Wales. Part of the problem is that the issues seem so abstract. This Enquiry therefore provides an innovative starting point for exploring the relations between England and Scotland.

It investigates the experiences of the Scottish and English people who inhabited the border territory.

While engaging pupils' interest in the *border reivers* and why they developed their distinctive customs (**Key Element 2b**), the unit also helps teachers to ensure that the unit includes proper attention to social and cultural diversity (**Key Element 2a**). Border people simply did not share many of the views and values of those elsewhere in Scotland and England. The Enquiry gradually reveals the roles of the monarchs in this wild way of life, offering the final twist that the very people who purported to be trying to control things, actually helped to sustain the violence.

> **Key terms**
> monarch, border, reiver, march, warden, custom, power, feud, kingdom

Extra access

Changing Minds Enquiry 5

Extra challenge

Low attainers often find it hard to move from describing historical situations to explaining them. **Copymaster 5.1** can be used in STEPs 1, 2 and 3 to help pupils to distinguish between describing and explaining the wildness of life in the borders.

Copymaster 5.2 offers extra advice on how to write the letter in 'Thinking your enquiry through'.

STEP 1
STEP 2
STEP 3

Thinking your enquiry through

Higher attainers will benefit from having the extra source material given in **Copymaster 5.3**. The references to the weaknesses of religion in border life are particularly significant and higher attainers should be able to express how shocking this would seem to an outsider in the 16th century.

Higher attainers should be required to use details from the textbook and from the extra sources to make their letter rich in period detail. A sign of higher attainment in exercises such as this is that the writing is historically grounded with plenty of precise information about who did what, when and where.

Extra access 5.1

Describing and explaining

You could use some of the these sentences to **explain** why life was wild in the borders. Colour these in red.

Some just help you to **describe** other things about life in the borders. Colour these in green.

STEP 1

> For hundreds of years Scottish and English families have been used to 'reiving' – making violent raids across the border.

> The lands around the border are called the marches.

> People sing songs about stealing.

> Everyone in the borders agrees that reiving is normal.

STEP 2

> One family is called the Armstrongs. Another is called the Grahams.

> Families can go on 'hot trods' – using force to win back their property as soon as it has been stolen.

> The men in charge of the borders are called wardens.

> Families often take violent revenge on each other even though they know this is not really allowed.

STEP 3

> Families are hard to control because the kings and queens of England and Scotland want them to be ready to fight at any moment.

> Many Scottish families hate other Scottish families – and many English families hate other English families.

> One warden came from France. He was called Anthony Darcy.

> One powerful Scottish family is called the Maxwells.

Making a letter better!

You have to write a letter to someone from outside the Scottish borders who is about to be made a warden. You have to warn the person to be careful. Why not learn from someone else's mistakes?

On this page you can see the letter which one school pupil wrote. You can also see the teacher's comments. Use this letter to help you to write an even better one! Try to do all the things the teacher suggests.

I really like this start. You sound so alarmed. Do this all the way through.

Dear new warden,

You mustn't come here to the Scottish borders. You really must not come. It is very dangerous here.

There are lots of powerful families here and they are very violent. They like to go reiving and no one can stop them. They have been doing this for hundreds of years.

This is all true. Well done. Could you explain what 'reiving' is and give some really horrible examples to worry the new warden? Tell him when they happened and who did what. (Pages 40 and 44 of Changing Minds have good examples.)

Something which makes life here even more dangerous is that the families are allowed to chase the people who have raided them and to win back their property. They do this a lot.

Good point. Why not say what they call this? You could explain how they used to take revenge as well. (See page 44 of Changing Minds.)

All the big families in the borders are always looking for trouble. They all seem to hate each other. Most of all they hate people from outside – like you! In 1516 they killed a warden called Anthony Darcy. I warn you not to come here.

From a worried friend.

Lots of good points. I think the new warden needs to know the names of some of these big families, don't you? And why not finish by telling him lots of nasty details about Anthony Darcy. Say what happened and when and why.

Good luck with your second attempt!

More information about the borders

One historian who has studied the Anglo-Scottish borders in great detail is George MacDonald Fraser. He wrote a book called *The Steel Bonnets* about life in the borders. You can see some extracts from this book below. Use information from these extracts in your letter to the new warden. Make sure you give him a lot to worry about!

In this extract Fraser describes the duties of a warden.

> A warden had to be a mixture of soldier, judge, lawyer, fighting-man, diplomat, politician, rough-rider, detective, administrator and intelligence agent. His duties were to guard the frontier, to confer with his opposite warden regularly, to supervise strongholds, suppress crime, pursue fugitives, hold courts, gather men for the defence of the march as required and generally keep good rule.
>
> In spite of all this the fact was that a warden could take the law into his own hands and go raiding and pillaging like any common reiver.

In this extract Fraser sums up the early career of one Scottish warden by the age of 26.

> By 1597, Robert Kerr was to be credited with sixteen killings and his raids were reckoned to have cost the English Marches over £60,000. And he was a warden of the marches.

In this extract Fraser shows how wardens often turned against each other.

> In midsummer of 1596, Scrope (English West) was on good terms with Johnstone (Scottish West), but on bad terms with Buccleuth (Liddesdale). Eure (English Middle) was on bad terms with Johnstone, but friendly with Buccleuth, although he did not expect the friendship to last long. Cessford (Scottish Middle) was friendly to Eure, but was 'displeased' with Robert Carey (English East).

In this extract Fraser gives another possible reason for life being so wild in the borders.

> It was natural in the climate of the times to blame lack of religion for much of the evil along the frontier. 'Want of knowledge of God, whereby the better sort forget oath and duty' was condemned by one English warden called Lord Eure. He saw churches 'mostly ruined to the ground, ministers and techers refusing to com and remaine where such heathenish people are'. There is no doubt that the Church suffered along with the ordinary people – one tradition credits the Armstrongs alone with the destruction of 52 church buildings.
>
> The religious failures of the Borderers seem to have been more or less permanent. The Scots Privy Council in 1602 were only echoing scores of earlier pronouncements when they attributed frontier disorders to the 'want of preiching of the word so that no small number of personis hes rune louse to all kynd of villainie and mischief'. In the area as a whole Redesdale and Tynedale were particularly irreligious, and at one time received only one church service per annum, from the courageous priest Bernard Gilpin.

From George MacDonald Fraser, The Steel Bonnets (Pan, 1974)

'Revenge for revenge and blood for blood'

Chopping and changing

What happened when Henry VIII took control of the Church?

Despite the 'What happened …' in its sub-title, this Enquiry is more than a mere narrative. The pupils are engaged in building a narrative but they must also explain cause and consequence (**Key Element 2b**). The consequences of the Break with Rome are very important in explaining so much in this period of history, so this Enquiry links with many others. Teachers will also want to make links back to the medieval period and the power of the Roman Catholic Church and early challengers such as the Lollards (**Key Element 2c**). Revisiting the Enquiry at the end of the whole unit would allow pupils to assess the significance of the Break with Rome within and beyond the period 1500 to 1750.

The final activity requires pupils to make the complex story very simple and clear for an audience of primary school children. This particular audience and form of writing helps to concentrate pupils' minds on the central points (**Key Element 5c**).

An important theme through the Enquiry is the unpredictability of events. Higher attainers should be expected to make more of this theme and opportunities exist for discussions on *counter factual history* by asking 'What if …'.

⚬—┓ Key terms
cause, consequence, Protestant, Roman Catholic

Extra access ❯

Changing Minds Enquiry 6

❮ Extra challenge

Copymaster 6.1 provides pupils with a ready-made chart for use with STEP 1. It also contains line drawings of Henry's reasons for wanting the divorce and the Break with Rome. These direct low attainers to the relevant parts of the Enquiry in STEP 1 and may be used in the final booklet that they are to prepare in 'Thinking your enquiry through'.

Copymaster 6.2 gives some suggestions for drawings to be done in STEP 2 and provides the chart for STEP 3.

STEP 1

STEP 2

STEP 3

Thinking your enquiry through

Higher attainers should be challenged at each STEP to include as much detail as possible – but in a concise style appropriate to the audience of a primary school class.

Copymaster 6.3 involves higher attainers in understanding the expression *Turning Point* and challenges them to define this. They must also select appropriate examples from a table of rebellions to show how the Break with Rome had long-term consequences.

High attainers could also be challenged to use and support the phrase *long-term causes* by making explicit links back to earlier work on religion in the Middle Ages.

The causes

Use this table to write down your reasons why Henry VIII made the Break with Rome.

STEP 1	The causes – Why Henry VIII made the Break with Rome
Love	
Money	
Faith	
Power	

These pictures may remind you why Henry wanted to break away from the Roman Catholic Church. You could use some or all of these pictures in your booklet when you explain the reasons.

The change and the consequences

Here are the boxes for your drawings about how Henry made the Break with Rome. Underneath you can read some suggestions for drawings. Decide which one could be used in which box – and then do your picture in the right place. (Use your own ideas if you prefer.)

Henry used Parliament to help him.

Henry put himself in charge of the Church.

Henry executed people who stayed loyal to the Church.

Henry closed all the monasteries and took their riches.

Suggestions for drawings (choose four):

- A church with a crown on top of its tower
- An axe
- A chained door with a sign saying 'Closed Forever'
- A crowd of rich men around the king on his throne
- A king with a sack of gold
- A parchment with 'New Laws' written on it

STEP 3

Use this table to write down the consequences of the Break with Rome.

What Henry wanted	What Henry did	What went wrong for Henry
Love	He married Anne Boleyn …	but _____ _____
Money	He closed all the monasteries and took their riches …	but _____ _____ _____
Faith	He _____ _____	but his new Church was more Protestant than he really wanted.
Power	He gave English monarchs power over a Protestant country …	but _____ _____ _____

The long-term view

1 The Break with Rome was a really important change in British history. For hundreds of years before it happened, England had been Roman Catholic. Henry ended this and for almost every single year since then England has been a Protestant nation. When such a big change happens at one time, historians call it a **Turning Point**. It is as if events have been travelling in one direction … and then they suddenly head off in a completely different direction!

In your booklet about the Break with Rome, write a clear explanation of why we could call the Break with Rome a **Turning Point** and design a simple diagram to illustrate what this means.

2 In your booklet you have to explain the consequences of Henry's Break with Rome. The chart below shows that his decision had consequences which affected the country for hundreds of years. We call these **long-term consequences**.

Study the table carefully. Make sure you are clear how the Break with Rome had long-term consequences for British history. Then explain what this means in your booklet and use two or three examples to prove that Britain was still affected by Henry's decision many years later.

Date	Event
1549	Catholics in Devon and Cornwall led a rebellion against the Protestant king, Edward VI.
1553–58	Mary I turned England Catholic again and burnt hundreds of English Protestants.
1558–1603	In the reign of Elizabeth I, who was a Protestant, there were many Catholic plots to kill her.
1588	The King of Spain sent the Spanish Armada to try to turn England Catholic again. It failed.
1605	Catholic plotters, including Guy Fawkes, planned to blow up the Protestant King James I and his Parliament.
1688	In the Glorious Revolution, Protestants in England forced the Catholic King James II to leave England. The Protestant King William and Queen Mary took over.
1690	Catholics in Ireland started a rebellion to win back the throne for James II. They failed.
1715	Catholics in Scotland started a rebellion to turn the United Kingdom Catholic again. They failed.
1745	Catholics in Scotland started another rebellion to turn the United Kingdom Catholic again. They failed.

Queen and country

How did Elizabeth control her people?

This Enquiry allows Key Stage 3 teachers to build on pupils' knowledge of the story of the Armada, making links back to Key Stage 2, Life in Tudor Times (**Key Element 2c**). The familiar Armada story and England's rivalry with Spain is used here to make a deeper point about the way monarchs ruled (i.e. letting an overview emerge from a depth study).

Pupils get inside the mind of those in power by taking the role of Elizabeth's Privy Councillors (**Key Element 2a**). They must make judgements based on contextual knowledge and then learn from the queen's actual actions. They then generalise on the basis of specific instances from Elizabeth's reign and give advice to the new king (**Key Element 5a**).

This link to the Stuarts can be picked up in Enquiry 8, especially the references to Parliament and taxation. The final activity can be written formally or spoken with the aid of notes (**Key Element 5c**). The STEPs convey an important learning message by requiring pupils to look at both sides of a problem before reaching their conclusion.

O┓ **Key terms**
Armada, Privy Council, Justice of the Peace, plot, traitor, monopoly, propaganda

---

Extra access

Copymaster 7.1 helps low attainers to weigh up the pros and cons of each decision in STEPs 1, 2, 3 and 4. It also helps pupils in 'Thinking your enquiry through' as it records some of the main difficulties faced by Elizabeth which are worth mentioning to the new king.

The final activity requires pupils to scan through the whole Enquiry for information. To help low attainers, **Copymaster 7.2** summarises what their speech to the king must say and helps them to find relevant points.

Changing Minds Enquiry 7

STEP 1

STEP 2

STEP 3

STEP 4

Thinking your enquiry through

Extra challenge

Higher attainers should be expected at each STEP to consider not just the specific short-term problem given to them but its wider significance (i.e. they should say why it is so important to get each decision right). This will deepen their understanding of constitutional issues, which this Enquiry is really about.

When preparing their speeches in 'Thinking your enquiry through', high attainers should consider **Copymaster 7.3** which gives further information and examples about the work of Privy Councillors and leads pupils into a deeper understanding of what qualities were needed in the advisers and in the monarch.

Weighing up the ideas

Privy councillors needed to **weigh up** their ideas before giving advice to Queen Elizabeth I. You should do the same in each STEP.

Give each sentence below a score. Use this scoring system:
1 = not important, 2 = quite important, 3 = important, 4 = very important. Count up the total on each side and then write down what you will tell the queen to do.

STEP 1

Tell Elizabeth to marry Philip because ...

Philip is rich and powerful. ☐

Philip could help England win its war against France. ☐

Tell Elizabeth not to marry Philip because ...

Philip is a Roman Catholic. ☐

Most English people hate Philip. ☐

I have decided to tell Elizabeth _____

STEP 2

Tell Elizabeth to execute Mary, Queen of Scots because ...

Spies and JPs tell you that Catholics are trying to put Mary, Queen of Scots on the English throne. ☐

Spies have proof that Mary is plotting against Elizabeth. ☐

Tell Elizabeth to keep Mary, Queen of Scots alive because ...

Mary says she has done nothing wrong. ☐

Powerful catholic countries like Spain will be very angry if Mary is executed. ☐

I have decided to tell Elizabeth _____

STEP 3

Tell Elizabeth to keep sailors on board their ships because ...

You do not know whether the Armada will return. ☐

The Lords Lieutenant tell you that they have only got weak armies on land to defend the coast. ☐

Tell Elizabeth to send the sailors home because ...

It costs a lot to pay their wages. ☐

God is on England's side and He will protect the country. ☐

I have decided to tell Elizabeth _____

STEP 4

Tell Elizabeth to keep using monopolies because ...

Kings and queens always need more money. ☐

Monopolies let Elizabeth get money without using Parliament – and she does not like to use Parliament very much. ☐

Tell Elizabeth to give up monopolies because ...

Monopolies put prices up and make people angry. ☐

People say monopolies are like an extra tax that doesn't have Parliament's permission. ☐

I have decided to tell Elizabeth _____

Advising the new king

Use the table below to plan what you will say to the new king.

What I want to prove to James I	Information which proves I am right – and where I can find it	What I'll say to James I
I want him to know that it is very difficult to rule England well.	**Marriage problems** – STEP 1 and pages 57–58 **Religion and plots** – STEP 2 and pages 58–59 **Wars** – STEP 3 and pages 57, 60–61 **Parliament and money** – STEP 4 and page 62	-- -- -- -- -- -- -- -- --
There are things which may help James I to rule England. He can rule well if he uses all the help available.	**The Privy Council** – page 57 **Justices of the Peace and Lords Lieutenant** – pages 58 and 60 **The navy** – page 60 **Parliament** – page 62 **Propaganda and God's support** – pages 60 and 63	-- -- -- -- -- -- -- --

Extra
challenge
7.3

**Thinking
your
enquiry
through**

The importance of the Privy Council

When you make your speech to King James I, you will want him to know how helpful the Privy Councillors can be. On this sheet are two sources which should help you to know more about the Privy Council. Use ideas from these in your speech to King James.

1 Queen Elizabeth's words to Sir William Cecil when she made him a Privy Councillor in 1558.

> I give you this charge that you shall be of my Privy Council and content yourself to make pains for me and my realm. I judge that you will not be corrupted with any manner of gift, and that you will be faithful to the state and that, without any fear of my private will, you will give me the advice that you think best. If you know anything to be declared to me in secret, you shall show it to myself only and assure yourself that I will not fail to keep that secret.

2 A modern historian, J B Black, writes about the Privy Council in the reign of Queen Elizabeth I.

> Its meetings were held in secret and were attended by eight or ten members. The queen never attended but let her wishes be known through the secretary [*William Cecil*] who was in constant communication with her. Normally she accepted the council's decisions but she did not regard herself as bound to follow its advice, nor did she hesitate to exercise an over-riding authority if she thought her own or national interests demanded it.
>
> There was always a rivalry among the members for a leading place in the queen's favour. Knowledge, as well as wisdom, was essential for anyone who aimed at taking a leading part in a debate. All the great figures of the Elizabethan council – William Cecil, Walsingham, Leicester, Essex, Robert Cecil – spared themselves no effort to acquire by an elaborate system of espionage, every scrap of information likely to be of use to them. As a rule Elizabeth respected the man whose opinions were based upon a rational analysis of the facts. A more vigilant, hard-working and loyal body of men than the Privy Council in Elizabeth's reign it would be hard to find.

From J B Black, The Reign of Elizabeth 1558–1603 *(Oxford, 1985)*

'A thing most horrible' ⑧

How did Charles I lose control?

The main focus of this Enquiry is cause (**Key Element 2b**) but presenting the information as a play lets personal attitudes and beliefs come through strongly (**Key Element 2a**). This is in keeping with the opening page which stresses the confusion and pain involved in civil war. By the end of the Enquiry, however, pupils can broaden their view of causation so that they sort out many different types of cause, for example political, religious, economic (**Key Element 5a**).

The STEPs are used to reinforce key points in the play and require pupils to match sources with events and dates (**Key Element 1a**). The reasons on page 73 are reproduced as cards on **Copymaster 8.1**. The relevant cards could be issued as each STEP is tackled, and pupils could be asked to find which part of the play matches the words on the card just as they are matching the pictures in each STEP. Other ways of sorting the cards are: chronologically, by long-, medium- and short-term causes, by individuals, by finding ones which can be used to blame Charles or Parliament. Discussion and evaluation of such arrangements involves pupils in important work on interpretations (**Key Element 3b**).

> **Key terms**
> civil war, Parliament, tax, Puritan

Extra access

The STEPs are relatively simple and are aimed at getting pupils to familiarise themselves with key events in the *story* of what led up to the war. This is important as the play uncovers layers of causation as it proceeds and low attainers may be confused if key people and events are not given due emphasis.

Copymaster 8.1 provides pupils with the reasons on cards shown at the end of the Enquiry. These should be cut up and sorted as directed in 'Thinking your enquiry through'.

Copymaster 8.2 provides ready-made circles for sorting the reasons in 'Thinking your enquiry through'. It may need to be enlarged for easiest use.

Changing Minds Enquiry 8

STEP 1

STEP 2

STEP 3

Thinking your enquiry through

Extra challenge

There is a lot of sophisticated thinking involved in sorting the cards on page 73 effectively – especially if higher attainers think creatively when suggesting their own ways of categorising causes. At the end, high attainers could be asked to write a commentary on their chart explaining what it tells us about the causes of the Civil War and/or about historical causation in general (i.e. webs of causation).

Copymaster 8.3 introduces higher attainers to the historiographical debate about the relative importance of individuals and broader social forces in bringing about change in history.

Sorting the reasons

Cut out these cards and use them to help you to sort out the reasons why the English Civil War broke out.

Thinking your enquiry through

James I taught his son Charles that God had given him power to rule alone.

Charles wanted more money.

Elizabeth I had been an inspiring leader and her people respected her.

Charles used fines and Ship Money to raise money without Parliament.

Parliament had become more powerful under the Tudors.

Archbishop Laud tried to end Puritan ideas in the Church of England.

Traders and landowners had grown rich since Tudor times and they wanted more power.

Parliament executed Strafford and arrested Archbishop Laud and blamed them for all the trouble.

Parliament kept trying to cut King Charles' power during the first three years of his reign.

Scottish rebels who hated Laud's new Prayer Book attacked England, so Charles had to call Parliament to raise money.

Puritan MPs were upset when Charles married a Catholic princess from France.

Charles forced his way into the House of Commons but failed to arrest five leading MPs.

Charles decided to rule without Parliament when it would not give him the taxes he wanted.

Charles left London and called all loyal subjects to join him in a war against Parliament's supporters.

The unpopular Earl of Strafford had a lot of power when Charles ruled without Parliament.

Parliament cut King Charles' power and refused to let him lead an army against Catholic rebels in Ireland.

Which reason fits where?

Use this diagram to sort out which reason fits where.

Thinking your enquiry through

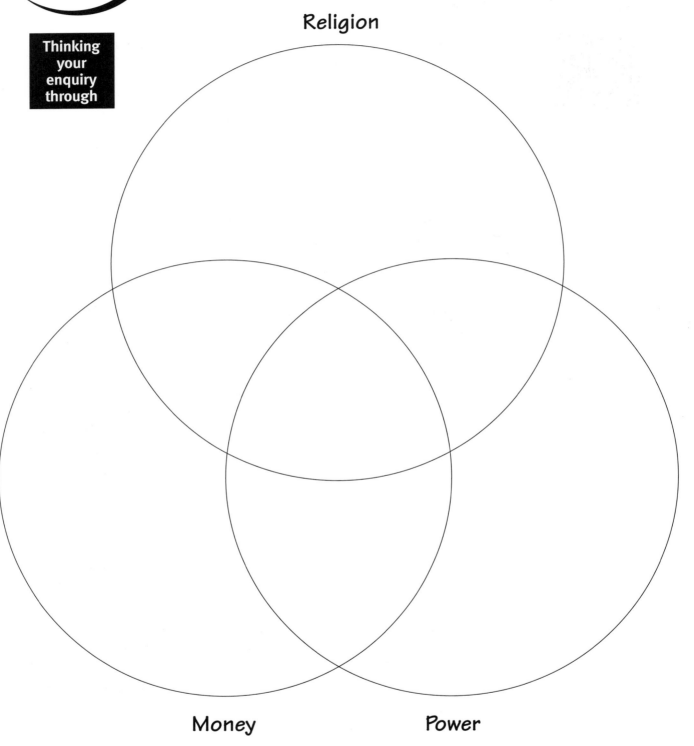

Religion

Money   Power

Historians disagree

Historians have had many disagreements about the English Civil War. They have given different interpretations about why it happened. Here are two examples.

A C V Wedgewood argues that the actions of individuals, especially Charles I, caused the Civil War.

> King Charles was serious-minded but he was not industrious. His casual attitude to his council, his unwillingness to listen to disturbing information, his hunting three or four times a week, the long hours spent in discussions about religion – all tell the same tale. He was not interested in practical administration [*running the country*]. He idled away the opportunities of his reign.

B Christopher Hill argues that it was changes in the whole of society that caused the Civil War.

> The causes of the Civil War must be found in society, not in individuals. A victory for Charles I and his gang could only have meant the economic stagnation of England … Each class created and sought to impose the religious views best suited to its own needs and interests. But the real clash is between these class interests.

1 Which of the reasons on page 73 of *Changing Minds* would each of these two historians use to back up their interpretation of the causes of the Civil War?

2 Look through the play in *Changing Minds*, Enquiry 8. Note down any references to individuals or social changes which helped to cause the war which the reasons on page 73 of *Changing Minds* do not mention.

3 Whose interpretation of the causes of the war do you think is most helpful? Explain your answer. You may want to suggest a better interpretation of your own.

'The maddest world we ever saw'

What made Britain seem so out of control between 1642 and 1660?

This Enquiry gives an overview of the years between 1642 and 1660, seen through the eyes of those at the time who felt this was 'the maddest world we ever saw'. It helps pupils to see the Civil War and Interregnum as a time when the complex network of society was out of joint (**Key Element 2a**). While certain aspects of life seemed *mad* to many people at the time, teachers will want to emphasise that these features do not all strike us as *mad* today. Indeed, some aspects which appeared *mad* to many at the time (e.g. the democratic ideas of the Levellers) have now become the norm. There is room for good citizenship work in the Enquiry.

Sections could be allocated for groupwork, with each group producing its own cartoon at the end and reporting back on the *madness* which people at the time may have perceived. This exercise shows pupils how cartoons exaggerate to convey a strong message. They have seen several examples of this throughout the Enquiry (**Key Element 4a**). For pupils who dislike drawing, a valid alternative is suggested.

As with all the Enquiries in *Changing Minds*, there is enough structure in this Enquiry to turn the final activity into an essay task if preferred.

Key terms

Roundhead, Parliamentarian, Cavalier, Royalist, New Model Army, republic, Commonwealth, Lord Protector, cartoon

---

Extra access

Changing Minds Enquiry 9

Extra challenge

Low attainers need to establish what most people expected their world to be like in the mid 16th century before they can assess what seemed *mad* at the time. **Copymaster 9.1** could well be used after reading about 'Your enquiry' at the very start. Matching the pictures with the words will reinforce the key points.

Copymaster 9.2 provides low attainers with a list of facts from the Enquiry. At each of STEPs 1, 2 and 3, pupils decide how *mad* each fact probably seemed at the time.

In 'Thinking your enquiry through', each pupil could do a cartoon about a different idea from the list, making a wall display about the 'Maddest world'.

Introduction

STEP 1

STEP 2

STEP 3

Thinking your enquiry through

This is a huge area of enquiry and could well be opened up for further research by high attainers. The focus on what made the world seem *mad* should be sustained.

Before doing the cartoon (or essay, see notes above) in the final activity, high attainers could be asked to rank order their lists completed in STEPs 1, 2 and 3 of what made the world seem *mad*.

The famous cartoon of 'The world turn'd upside down' at the start of the Enquiry is full of little details. High attainers should be challenged to include similar details in their own cartoon.

Another extension task would be to ask high attainers to write a commentary explaining a class display about the 'Maddest world' and the references it is making.

Life before the 'madness'

Before you can spot what seemed **mad** to ordinary people between 1642 and 1660, you may need to remind yourself of what most people thought was **normal** in those times.

Each sentence below tells you what most people believed about the way life should be before 1642. Cut out the pictures from the bottom of the sheet and stick each one into a box above the right sentence.

Every country should be ruled by a king or queen.

Ordinary people enjoyed all sorts of simple entertainments especially on religious holidays and on Sundays.

MPs were all rich, educated men. No one thought that poor people or women should vote or be MPs.

Everyone was expected to follow the same religion (Church of England).

Poor people had to look up to the king and to rich people with great respect.

All men should fight for their king when he ordered them to.

No one should ever fight against the king.

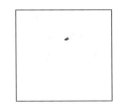

Parliament was full of rich, sensible Lords and MPs who helped the king by advising him and making laws.

'The maddest world we ever saw'

Some events from the 'maddest world we ever saw'

Read each of the facts. Next to each one, shade in the correct number of dots to show how **mad** each fact probably seemed to ordinary people at the time. (Remember to use the work you did on **Copymaster 9.1** to remind you what people expected in those days.)

A little bit mad ● ○ ○ ○
Completely mad ● ● ● ●

Try to add an extra fact of your own to each list.

STEP 1

The two sides in the Civil War called each other **Roundheads** and **Cavaliers.** ○ ○ ○ ○

Parts of the country kept changing hands during the war. ○ ○ ○ ○

Fathers fought against their own sons in bloody battles. ○ ○ ○ ○

Some women joined the armies. ○ ○ ○ ○

_____ ○ ○ ○ ○

STEP 2

King Charles was put in prison by his own people. ○ ○ ○ ○

King Charles was put on trial for treason. ○ ○ ○ ○

King Charles was executed. ○ ○ ○ ○

Levellers said everyone over 21 (except women and servants) should be allowed to vote. ○ ○ ○ ○

Quakers said violence is always wrong. ○ ○ ○ ○

_____ ○ ○ ○ ○

STEP 3

From 1649 to 1658 Oliver Cromwell had more power than anyone else in Britain. ○ ○ ○ ○

In 1653 Cromwell used soldiers to close Parliament down. ○ ○ ○ ○

Puritans closed all theatres and banned dancing round maypoles. ○ ○ ○ ○

_____ ○ ○ ○ ○

Monarchs in their place

Who had control after 1660?

This Enquiry uses the idea of monarchs maintaining or losing their power to produce an overview of the shifting balance of political control between 1660 and 1750 (**Key Element 2c**). The content and ideas are lightened and made more accessible by allowing the monarchs to speak for themselves. (Six different pupils could each be asked to read the words of the monarch to emphasise their contrasting characters.)

The preoccupations of monarchs at the time should emerge, for example Parliament, money, religion, and war.

The balloon debate is an oral activity which is based on secure knowledge (**Key Element 5c**). This knowledge should be ensured by the STEPs.

A further dimension can be added to the debate if, for example, the higher attainers within a group are given the extra job of studying the other monarchs and attacking their claims, always keeping to the facts provided.

Key terms
monarch, Republic, rebellion, Glorious Revolution, Bill of Rights, Prime Minister

---

Extra access

Copymaster 10.1 helps low attainers with each of STEPs 1, 2 and 3. It gives simple pictures and bullet point summaries of each monarch. For each one, low attainers must decide which bullet point is the most important and highlight it. They then say why that point seemed to be so important.

Copymaster 10.2 can be used in two ways. The score sheet gives all pupils hints about what the judges are looking for. In this way, it helps pupils at each STEP to select the best material to say why each monarch should stay in the balloon. (Unlikely to be used in addition to 10.1.) More simply, it can be used by the judges to keep their scores as each monarch speaks about why he or she should stay in the balloon in 'Thinking your enquiry through'.

Changing Minds Enquiry 10

STEP 1
STEP 2
STEP 3

Extra challenge

At each STEP high attainers could be asked to gather extra facts which they will use to attack the credentials of the other monarchs in the balloon debate.

Alternatively, higher attainers could take the role of the judges. They will need to explain to the monarchs in the balloon why the criteria for throwing a monarch out are relevant and why they gave each monarch the score they did.

Holding power ... or losing power?

In the boxes below you can see the six monarchs (kings or queens) who are mentioned in Enquiry 10. Below each one you will see four sentences describing what the monarch did. Underline the sentence which you think is most important. Then write a sentence of your own. Say why you think this king or queen was still well in control or was losing power.

Charles II
- Parliament offered me the crown.
- I had all the same powers my father had when he was king.
- I didn't have enough money.
- I ruled without Parliament for four years.

_____

_____

_____

James II
- I had enough money to rule.
- I crushed the Duke of Monmouth's rebellion.
- I upset Parliament by giving the best jobs to my Catholic friends.
- I ran away to France when Parliament asked William and Mary to invade.

_____

_____

_____

William III
- Parliament asked me and my wife to be king and queen.
- Parliament limited my power by passing a Bill of Rights.
- I defeated James II and Catholic rebels in Ireland in 1690.
- I worked very hard.

_____

_____

_____

Anne
- Some people said I was not very clever.
- I let my friends rule the country.
- I always used Parliament to help me rule.
- I was the first monarch to have England and Scotland ruled by the same Parliament in London.

_____

_____

_____

George I
- I spent as much time as possible in Hanover.
- I let Robert Walpole have a lot of power in Parliament.
- I made sure the king could always choose his ministers.
- Britain was rich and peaceful when I died.

_____

_____

_____

George II
- Robert Walpole promised me lots of money.
- Parliament forced me to have ministers I did not want.
- My army crushed the Scottish rebels in 1745.
- I ruled for 33 years.

_____

_____

_____

Extra access 10.2

Judging the monarchs

Use this copymaster to make simple notes about each monarch. The headings tell you what a monarch needs to do well.

STEPS 1, 2, 3	Charles II	James II	William III
Personality A good monarch is decisive and strong			
Parliament A good monarch must avoid quarrels with Parliament			
Religion A good monarch avoids problems here or acts quickly to end them			
Wars A good monarch needs to win battles and wars			
Money A good monarch has enough money to run the country			

	Anne	George I	George II
Personality A good monarch is decisive and strong			
Parliament A good monarch must avoid quarrels with Parliament			
Religion A good monarch avoids problems here or acts quickly to end them			
Wars A good monarch needs to win battles and wars			
Money A good monarch has enough money to run the country			

Forcing minds to change

1547 to 1603:
When was it most dangerous to speak your mind?

Religious changes during the Tudor and Stuart period sometimes seem very hard to teach. *Changing Minds* tackles this in a number of ways:

1 Enquiry 11 offers an overview of changes from the time of Edward VI's reign through to 1603. It concentrates upon the core issues and revisits them through the course of the Enquiry. It uses the theme of danger and culminates in a motivating activity (the Danger Chart) to help pupils to see the importance of changing religious beliefs (**Key Elements 2a, 2b and 2d**).

2 Other Enquiries, notably 6, 7, 8 and 13, also address religious issues, often using smaller stories. This revisiting across the period helps pupils to get to grips with the religious mindset of the period in a variety of social and political contexts.

3 Enquiry 11 also offers a European context for the religious changes, expanding the pupils' frame of reference and helping them to make links as required by **Key Element 2c**.

Teachers can assess pupils' knowledge and understanding of the religious changes by the information they select and deploy on their Danger Charts.

O—⚷ Key terms

Protestant, Roman Catholic, Church, Christian, priest, Pope, Mass, reformer, persecution, Puritan, monarch

---

Extra access

Changing Minds Enquiry 11

Extra challenge

Copymaster 11.1 helps low attainers by establishing the differences between Roman Catholic and Protestant views. It is a good idea to use it after 'Making the changes 1' and before STEP 1.

Copymaster 11.2 builds on 11.1. The date in each sentence helps pupils to find the right reign in *Changing Minds* and to check what happened to Catholics and/or Protestants at that time. They can then use this knowledge to make their table of dangers and to explain their choices.

Low attainers can use the sentences on **Copymaster 11.2** as the basis for their Danger guides to put on their Danger Chart in 'Thinking your enquiry through'.

STEP 1

STEP 2

Thinking your enquiry through

Copymaster 11.3 presents a modern historian's summary of the religious shifts across and within the reigns of Edward VI, Mary I and Elizabeth I. High attainers should be expected to use this to add extra details to their tables of dangers at each STEP and to position their cards with greater precision in 'Thinking your enquiry through'.

Extra access 11.1

Introduction

Catholic and Protestant ... spot the difference

On the right you can see a Protestant. On the left you can see a Roman Catholic.

1 Read the speech bubbles.

2 Underline any words which are clues to show whether the speech bubble is coming from the Protestant or from the Roman Catholic.

3 Draw a line from each bubble to the correct person.

> I believe that the church must be very simple with no crosses or candles. People must understand the truth about God by reading the Bible for themselves. We must get rid of old, superstitious ideas about God and try to keep things simple and clear.

> I believe that the old ways of the church are best. We must obey the Pope. God is a great mystery. We need priests to give us God's forgiveness. They help us to worship Him in beautiful buildings and to pray in the lovely Latin language.

Dangerous words!

Use this copymaster and other ideas from *Changing Minds* pages 95 to 100 to help you to make your tables of danger in STEP 1 and STEP 2.

In the bubbles below you can read some words spoken by English Catholics and Protestants between 1549 and 1603.

1 In the space provided below each bubble, write down whose reign each one is in. The dates will help you.

2 Next to each bubble write a number from 1 to 5 to show how much danger the person would be in at that time. (1 = very safe, 5 = very dangerous)

I am a Protestant in 1557. I want to worship in English and to read the Bible in English with my friends.

I am a Catholic bishop in 1550. I like the old ways of running the Church.

I am a rich Catholic in 1562. I do not go to church.

I am a Puritan in 1575. I try to live a good life – but I don't go around telling others to copy me.

I am a Catholic priest in 1581. I want to help Catholics to worship properly.

I am a Puritan in 1583. I want church people to choose their own leaders.

I am a Catholic in 1551. In my village we still use the old Catholic ways. No one has noticed yet!

Making your Danger Chart really accurate

Enquiry 11 in *Changing Minds* has shown you that, if a Protestant was on the throne, the Catholics were in danger; if a Catholic was on the throne, the Protestants were in danger. But – like most things in history – it was more complicated than that!

In the passage below, a modern historian explains what changed within each reign between 1549 and 1603. Read it carefully. Use this extra information to make your Danger Chart really accurate. You could include some advice which starts, 'If you thought it was safe to be a rich Catholic at the start of Elizabeth's reign – watch out! Things have changed now ...'

Under King Edward VI, Cranmer's new Book of Common Prayer in English was introduced in 1549. It was a careful mix of old and new. It was written in English but it did follow many Catholic traditions and forms of worship. By 1552 Cranmer had revised it and made it more Protestant than it had been in 1549. The country was becoming more and more Protestant as the reign continued.

When Mary I took the throne in 1553, she saw it as her mission to lead her people back to the true ways of the Roman Catholic faith. Her government encouraged priests to use the old Catholic Mass as soon as she became queen. In the next six months, hundreds of Protestants fled to the continent to join Churches which followed the ideas of Calvin or Luther. Mary's government encouraged them to go and it was only later that she took serious action against those who stayed.

Mary had to wait until the end of 1554 before Parliament agreed to pass a law restoring the Pope's authority over the Church in England. From that time onwards she was more severe on Protestants. On 4 February 1555 the first Protestant martyr, John Rogers, was burnt at Smithfield. Some three hundred more were to follow before Mary herself died in 1558.

From the start of her reign in 1558, Queen Elizabeth I made great efforts to settle the country's religious problems by taking a middle way. For ten years or so it seemed to work well. Poor Catholics who could not afford to pay the one shilling (5p) weekly fine for not attending church usually did as they were told. Richer Catholics stayed away from church but Elizabeth left them alone so long as they caused her no trouble. All seemed well, but it did not last.

In 1570 came a turning point. In that year the Pope announced that Catholics in England no longer needed to obey Elizabeth. He encouraged them to plot against her. Before long Elizabeth's spies were uncovering numerous Catholic plots to remove Elizabeth by force and to make Mary, Queen of Scots the new, Catholic queen of England. For the next twenty years the threat from Catholics grew – and Elizabeth had to use greater force against them. By 1585 Catholic priests and those who sheltered them were being put to death and the fine for non attendance at church went up to £20 a month so that even rich Catholics were now being forced to obey the laws of religion. It was in the last twenty years or so of Elizabeth's reign that about two hundred and fifty Catholics were put to death. In the first twenty years barely any had suffered in this way.

All this time another problem had been growing. Hundreds of Puritans had returned to England from the continent with high hopes when Elizabeth had become queen in 1558. They wanted her to transform the Church into one modelled on the ideas of John Calvin. It was not to be. By the 1580s these Puritans and others who followed their lead were pressing the queen to let the people choose their own church leaders. Elizabeth would have none of this. From 1589 onwards Puritans suffered attack after attack from the government. Many of their leaders were imprisoned and four were executed. In 1593 a fierce act promised to exile or execute all who refused to attend church or who attended unauthorised religious meetings.

Forcing minds to change

Culture clash

Why was there no meeting of minds in the New World?

This Enquiry considers the development of English colonies in North America by a series of case studies. Themes concerning the beliefs and behaviour of the colonists and of native Americans will emerge. This approach also encourages pupils to enter the mindset of the colonists and of the Native Americans. (**Key Element 2a**)

This is an important Enquiry for developing cultural understanding and moral sensitivity. Pupils should see how beliefs affect action (**Key Element 2b**).

The repetition of the questions in each STEP reinforces the learning.

Once again (as with all Enquiries in the Think Through History series) the final activity is training pupils in the ability to sort and structure information, so that they are left with the framework for extended writing. Pupils should be encouraged to group their ideas sensibly. Some teachers may wish pupils to go further and write an actual essay.

Key terms
culture, Native Americans, New World, trade, colonist

Extra access

Copymaster 12.1 can be used in STEP 1 and STEP 2 to help low attainers to answer the questions.

Copymaster 12.2 continues the same support, this time for STEP 3.

Copymaster 12.2 also provides a picture which can be used as the basis for the activity in 'Thinking your enquiry through'.

Changing Minds Enquiry 12

STEP 1
STEP 2
STEP 3
Thinking your enquiry through

Extra challenge

Copymaster 12.3 gives higher attainers a modern historian's account of relations between natives and settlers. This can be used at each STEP to add extra depth to pupils' understanding of the differences between the Native Americans and the colonists.

In 'Thinking your enquiry through', high attainers should be encouraged to sort their ideas so that they organise their reasons for the culture clash into categories rather than just putting them in a random order.

Culture clash – 1

The tables below help you to answer the questions in STEPs 1 and 2. The top row is complete. It has the question on the left. In the middle are some useful words. On the right is a short clear answer which uses the key words.

Fill in any empty boxes by using the useful words you have been given or by choosing some useful words from the answer shown.

STEP 1

Question	Key words	Answer
Why did the colonists go to the New World?	find out first	Raleigh's men went to Roanoke in 1585 because he wanted to find out about the New World and he wanted the English to be the first Europeans to take land in North America.
What did they do when they got there?	drew traded built land	_____ _____ _____ _____ _____
Why did they clash with the Native Americans?	_____ _____ _____	The English did not understand the Native American beliefs about land and sharing. They used force to take what they wanted.

STEP 2

Question	Key words	Answer
Why did the colonists go to the New World?	gold and silver	_____ _____ _____
What did they do when they got there?	_____ _____ _____ _____	They built a fort and stole food from the Native Americans. Later they took hunting land from the Native Americans and used it to grow tobacco which they sold in England.
Why did they clash with the Native Americans?	frightened too many English hunting murder	_____ _____ _____ _____

Culture clash

Extra access 12.2

Culture clash – 2

The table below helps you to answer the questions in STEP 3.
It has the question on the left.

STEP 3

Fill in any empty boxes by using the useful words you have been given or by choosing some useful words from the answer shown.

Question	Key words	Answer
Why did the colonists go to the New World?	- - - - - - - - - - - - - - - - - - - - - - - - - - - - - - - - - - - - - - - - - - - - - - - -	Many were Puritans who were running away from King James. They wanted to start a new 'godly' land in America.
What did they do when they got there?	built maize hunting fishing trade	- - - - -
Why did they clash with the Native Americans?	believed chosen by God use land	- - -

Thinking your enquiry through

Use this outline picture when you do your final task.

Native Americans
People cannot own the land.

_____
_____
_____
_____
_____

Colonists
We want to farm the land.

_____
_____
_____
_____
_____

Culture clash

The two cultures – an historian's view

Here is what the historian Hugh Brogan wrote about the meeting of the first European settlers and the Native Americans (he calls them 'Indians'). Use some of his comments to help you to give other examples of what caused the clash of the two cultures.

Indian tribes were commonly happy to fight each other. They had the usual human grievances against their neighbours, and war was a principal occupation among them. Success in war was the leading source of individual prestige. Indeed, before the Europeans' arrival, wars seem to have been waged in many cases solely to provide chances for warriors to win this prestige. The skill gained in this wilderness conflict proved invaluable for attacking or defending European possessions.

Names are revealing. What did the races call each other? The colonists had a long list of savoury adjectives and nouns for the Indians: for example childish, cruel, degraded, dirty, diseased, lazy, lying, murdering, stupid, thieving, barbarians, heathen, savages. The red men were no less definite. At first, by one group, the Europeans were called 'The People from Heaven'. Later Indians who came to know them well, dubbed them 'People Greedily Grasping for Land'. Members of the Algonquin group most commonly called the English 'The Coat Wearing People'; next often, 'The Cut-Throats'.

Indian technological backwardness was largely inevitable because of the absence in America of easily worked tin and iron deposits and of animals suitable for pulling heavy loads, which meant that the principle of the wheel could not be exploited.

The Europeans can hardly be blamed for spreading infections such as smallpox, cholera, measles and influenza. Nor should they all be condemned for the worst disease of all, alcoholism. Fermented and distilled drinks were unknown to the Indians, so they had as little resistance to alcoholism as to smallpox.

Indians were demons when on the warpath, but it should be observed that in their peacetime behaviour (unless upset by booze) they were, compared to the white men, models of good behaviour. Much about European manners astonished and distressed them. They could not understand child beating or exclusive family loyalty: 'I don't understand you Frenchmen, you love only your own children, but we love all children' said an Algonquin to a missionary.

The Indians shared what they had, especially food: it was noted that when there was any to share they all shared it; when there was none, all starved. Most of all they shared the land. Why did the People Greedily Grasping for Land want more acres than they needed to grow food on? Why did they build houses that would outlast the occupants? Why were Indians called thieves for helping themselves to what they needed as they always had?

Adapted from Hugh Brogan, The Penguin History of the USA *(Penguin, 1990)*

Evil on their minds

Why did people believe in witches?

The focus of this Enquiry is on the idea of a *witch-craze*. Teachers will want to ensure that this phrase is understood by pupils. The pupils' task involves understanding a mindset which is so different from that of our own world today (**Key Element 2a**).

The content and the sources are likely to be intrinsically interesting to most pupils. They must draw suitable examples from this material in each

STEP and then select and use these (**Key Element 5a**) to substantiate their ideas in an analytical essay (**Key Element 5c**).

The Enquiry offers teachers valuable opportunities to discuss social and moral issues, for example by considering whether the treatment of witches could be called *bullying*, or how easy/hard it is for individuals to stand against a social tide.

O—π Key terms
witch-craze, witchcraft, trial, familiars

Extra access

Changing Minds
Enquiry 13

Extra challenge

Copymaster 13.1 helps lower attainers at each of STEPs 1, 2 and 3 by giving them sentences with missing words. After reading the relevant section they should be able to select the best word(s) to fill each gap from the list provided. The second way in which it helps is by requiring low attainers to find a precise supporting detail to use in their essay in 'Thinking your enquiry through'.

STEP 1
STEP 2
STEP 3

Thinking your enquiry through

Copymaster 13.2 challenges higher attainers by giving them some extra contemporary sources about witchcraft. These can be used within STEPs 1, 2 and 3 as indicated on the sheet.

High attainers should be able to use precise details from Enquiry 11 and from **Copymaster 13.2** to support their arguments in 'Thinking your enquiry through'.

Why did people believe in witches?

Use words from the large box on the right to fill in the gaps in the sentences on the left. As you do this in each STEP, you are building up your list of reasons why people believed in witches.

STEP 1

_____ spread frightening ideas about witches.

Crowds of people watched witches being _____ .

_____ such as Henry VIII, Elizabeth I and James I all believed witches were dangerous.

New _____ were passed which made more people think witches were a really serious problem.

STEP 2

There were more witch trials at times when life was _____ .

There were lots of witch trials in areas controlled by the _____ who told people that witchcraft made God angry.

People thought that ordinary _____ were 'familiars' or evil spirits in disguise.

People often accused witches of causing alarming _____ and illnesses.

STEP 3

People believed witch-finders who said they could use _____ to prove that someone was a witch.

Many women confessed that they were witches at their _____ .

It was often rich people who _____ women of being witches.

accused
executed
laws
difficult
tests
Monarchs
pets
Puritans
Books
accidents
trials

Evil on their minds

More sources on witchcraft

Read the sources on this page and use them to suggest more reasons why so many people were ready to believe in witches in the 16th and 17th centuries. In particular, look for any signs of prejudice against certain types of person or behaviour.

1 From Archbishop Cranmer's *Articles of Visitation* which told senior priests what they should check for when they visit a parish. It was written in 1549.

> You shall inquire whether they know of any that use charms, sorcery, enchantments, soothsaying or any like craft invented by the devil.

2 From a sermon by Bishop Jewel preached to Queen Elizabeth I in 1558.

> Witches and sorcerers within these last few years are marvellously increased in Your Grace's realm. Your Grace's subjects pine away even unto their death, their colour fadeth, their flesh rotteth, their speech is benumbed, their senses are bereft. These eyes have seen most evident and manifest marks of the wickedness of these witches.

3 A description of the sort of woman who was most commonly accused of being a witch, written by John Gaule in 1646.

> Every old woman with a wrinkled face, a furrowed brow, a hairy lip, a gobber tooth, a squint eye, a squeaking voice or a scolding tongue, having a ragged coate upon her back, a skull-cap on her head, a spindle in her hand and a dog or a cat by her side is not only suspected but pronounced to be a witch.

4 An account of a witch at work adapted from *A treatise of Witchcraft* by Alexander Roberts. It was written in 1616.

> Mary Smith of King's Lynn envied her neighbours who made better cheese than she did. While she was angry, Satan came to her as a black man. She agreed to forsake God and follow the devil. She cursed one man and made his fingers rot off. She cursed a woman who she accused of stealing her hen. The woman went into a fit and tore the hair off her own head. Mary sent her imp – a toad – to crawl about the house of a man who made better cheese than she did. One of his servants took the toad and threw it into the fire which sent Mary into a terrible torment. In 1616 Mary Smith was found guilty of witchcraft and hanged by the neck until she was dead.

'Words new and unheard of'

How did ideas change when great minds went to work?

The focus of this Enquiry is on understanding the nature of the scientific way of thinking which developed in the 17th century (**Key Element 2a**). By taking four individuals as the basis, the ideas are rooted in story, which should avoid the problem of abstract scientific ideas dominating the Enquiry.

There is an element of a puzzle as pupils' search for new words within the Enquiry. The repetition of the need for new words means that the central idea of rapid progress in science is constantly reinforced.

The work of the final scientist (Savery) has a more technological emphasis and this makes this Enquiry suitable for linking forward to work on the Industrial Revolution (**Key Element 2c**).

The STEP activities require selection of relevant details (**Key Element 5a**). The final activity may seem very light in itself, but teachers will recognise that the chart actually provides pupils with an essay plan. Good discussion could take place about how to use it as a plan even if the essay is not actually written (feeding **Key Element 5c**).

> **Key terms**
> science, experiment, dome, microscope, cell, telescope, gravity, steam engine, horsepower

Extra access

Changing Minds Enquiry 14

Extra challenge

The main task in each STEP is very straightforward. Low attainers may need to be directed to specific paragraphs which concentrate on the particular achievements that must be mentioned. Information can be recorded on **Copymaster 14.1** which gives two empty factfiles.

When tackling the final activity in 'Thinking your enquiry through', low attainers will find it helpful to be told that there are several key words to look for when scanning their factfiles and/or the textbook. These are shown in the list on the left-hand side of the chart in **Copymaster 14.2**.

High attainers can be asked to carry out extra research into each of the four, named scientists. In particular, it would be worth asking pupils to check whether Sir Christopher Wren deserves to be called a scientist.

Copymaster 14.3 can be added as an extension to 'Thinking your enquiry through'. It asks high attainers to decide what criteria are most appropriate when deciding what makes a scientist important in the development of science. As an introduction to this, the teacher could suggest that Savery's work was more important than the others because it produced a useful machine. High attainers may enjoy attacking or defending this proposition.

Factfile sheets

STEPS 1, 2, 3, 4

Name: _____

Born: _____

Died: _____

Achievements (*Continue on the back of this sheet if necessary*): _____

_____

_____

_____

People who helped: _____

_____

New words he introduced: _____

Name: _____

Born: _____

Died: _____

Achievements (*Continue on the back of this sheet if necessary*): _____

_____

_____

_____

People who helped: _____

_____

New words he introduced: _____

What did scientists have in common?

	Wren	Hooke	Newton	Savery
'I used mathematical calculations in my work'				
'I was helped by the Royal Society'				
'I used microscopes or telescopes'				
'I got ideas from other countries in Europe'				
'I was really excited by all sorts of scientific work'				
'I had to introduce a new word'				

Extra
challenge
14.3

Thinking
your
enquiry
through

What makes a great scientist?

You have been looking for qualities that four early members of the Royal Society had in common. This sheet suggests many other qualities which these and other early scientists may have shown as they worked to develop science.

Read the list below carefully and decide which qualities you think were most important in helping the development of science. Choose your top five qualities and number each one in order of importance (1 is the top quality). Invent better ones of your own if you can. Discuss your choices with a partner.

- Used his ability and made one really great scientific breakthrough.

- Worked very hard to set up the Royal Society so that it lasted for hundreds of years.

- Was very hard working.

- Had the energy and interest to do a wide variety of scientific investigations.

- Made a really practical and useful invention which could be used to make things.

- Became famous in his own lifetime.

- Got on well with other scientists and worked closely with them.

- Made a fortune out of his scientific ability.

- Improved a piece of scientific equipment which later scientists used to make great discoveries.

- Raised lots of really interesting questions but could not answer them.

- Had the patience to carry on working when facing great difficulties.